Paring

poems by

Travis Chi Wing Lau

Finishing Line Press
Georgetown, Kentucky

Paring

ACKNOWLEDGMENTS

"Crabapple" was first published in *Impossible Archetype*, Issue 7.
"Still Life" and "Recovered: Vegetable Knife" were first published in *The South Carolina Review*, Volume 52.2.
"Gohyah Tea" was first published in *Poached Hare*, Issue 4.
"Snow Chrysanthemum" was first published in *Assaracus: A Journal of Gay Poetry*, Issue 21.

Publisher: Leah Maines
Editor: Christen Kincaid
Cover Art: Ann Lena Ho
Author Photo: Den Sweeney
Cover Design: Elizabeth Maines McCleavy

Order online: www.finishinglinepress.com
also available on amazon.com

Author inquiries and mail orders:
Finishing Line Press
P. O. Box 1626
Georgetown, Kentucky 40324
U. S. A.

Table of Contents

For all that never came to fruition.
For all that may still.

pare, v.

from the French *parer;* Latin *parare*

to adorn, beautify
to prepare, arrange
to pride oneself in, glory in
to peel, trim
to prune, shave
to produce, beget
to skin, reach the living beneath
to compare, be compared

Paring

He makes certain not to turn around as the
house recedes behind him into the same

horizon as the oak that should have died
in that frost when the caribou came, and

his father was too slow with the polaroid,
but he learned that the trick of survival is

stubbornness because the geraniums know
to live even when forgotten, even when a boy

leaves home for the first time and will forget
who he is before he remembers what he can be.

This is growing, yes, but it cannot only be exceeding
a mother's truisms made holy by rosary or

the fit of what was handed down by bone or
by blood, so he must do the work of paring

away the loyalties that have taken bitter root
down to browning cores that once kept him alive,

but stop the fruiting to maintain the skins,
so he pares and pares and pares until a single peel

reveals to him the myth of every
parent's flowering wish.

be sure to eat the skins

> *Skin, though it takes pains to remember caresses, is marked by*
> *the roads that pain takes.* —Rosemarie Waldrop

By the hand, she would lead me
        through the crowds of homemakers taking life into their hands
        to judge its fit for sustaining their own:
        the fragrant language of skins,
                touch and weight.

To tell bitterness before the taste
        can save, she instructs, with the certainty of callused palms
        that learned by needlework and scalding water what
        the labor of the eye can do even before the hand
        because the meeting of any two bodies is
                sacred.

Ritual: before the words, I learned to read skins
        for their wells of sharp truth sweetest
        when nearing fullness,
        when edging toward
                sugary rot.

How do you know the dew is honeyed, little one?
        Easy, you ask the skin
        with the gentle force of fingertips
        to confirm what the blossom end cannot help
                but betray.

Dull thud, a thump:
        a history of falls and no one to pick it up,
        yet bruising renders it no less worthy
        for what it will make of the flesh,
                the fruit.

You eat the skin
        because it is living memory,
        because it once was a shield,
        because it is so hastily stripped,
        because it is supposed to be
                good for you.

Ikebana

The fault is in the hesitation
               the force of inaction
unrelieved to the pitch
               of breakage
of oppression so familiar
               yet without a name
a theory of cutting
               clean like the cistern
holds its water
               until it cannot but
overflow into
               the immensity of a single
thought that braves
               a cicada's life
singing itself into being
               one man set boldly
before another
               until the next cut
preserves
               rather than kills
still still
               life
one joy placed
               beside another.

The Sick Rose
After William Blake

Peril is an intimacy, tightly coiled,
a way of safely occupying a fixed thing
when it wriggles, thrashes for the right to live
how it knows best (even if it is a self-
containment it cannot afford). It claims the
body as it tries to resolve itself with other
bodies: failed measures, a faulty kindling
in the interim—holding over that holds really
nothing but an inner flower left untasted behind
a guard of worms that reminds it where it came from
and where it will return. A bed of crimson joy,
spillage that does not destroy.

Seeded

take yourself up those groaning
steps yeah the ones that cling to your
feet because you know it's more
than a finish more than his
sly watching slick like your hands
a game of numbers it's one of those
nights to be braved fuck the cold snap
because he will hold you like he did
those blurry months ago when you were
here in the city of seedlings catching
eyes swift in flashes of limbs that feel
into the throaty dark you know that
place that gets caught in your throat
well after you get in the car with parting
gifts scrawled on post-its and thighs tight
and tender as so many of them were
tonight even the one in the corner who
never gets pulled into the knot that
takes hours to untie itself back into
straight lines prim and pressed for the
ride home to them because he didn't kiss
you and that's the one rule he made
even when you both bore a share of this
naked supper and may never again

Jasmine (I)

> *How wonderful it was this coming to know, certain of the knowing*
> *to come. Every word was weighted and every glance an inquiry.*
>
> —*Jamie O'Neill*

i.

Meeting was a prosecco's bite. Under the auspices
                                    of a coast still wintering, we shivered
to the falling sun indistinguishable
from the fizz of a laugh.

What defines the difference between
a wall falling or a jacket draping
over shoulders that know
                    ache over fit?

An arm, two breaths: what hovered before us in white butterflies,
                    what hushed into the night.

ii.

A man: makes lips to the steam uncurling pearls of jasmine.
A man: wraps two hands around a paper cup.

How much does it take for two broken men to walk upright?
A spine, a spirit: wanders,
                    but mostly to get away from itself.
Flee,
fleeing,
fled.

iii.

His legs yawned, so we walked among the marble giants.

A love for parallelism:
           line by line,
           side by side,   no intersection because that is forbidden
except in the form of accident.
           Collisions threaded by what his mother told him when
              he was unable to sit on her lap anymore.

iv.

Half-reclined in the passenger seat, I learned what could drive a man
to want to kill his breath.

Inspiration:
a refusal, then gasping.
(too late
too late)

Sighs that would one day need   to expire.

v.

In my hand was a ballpoint pen,
stolen
        from some headquarters
        five hundred miles away:
                what seeks refuge
                        stains hands.

(The rental car door
sounded different when
slammed shut,

        an accidental.)

vi.

The last I would see of him was when he asked to stop
               a pause
               for white stars

                         trained to thrive in
                         an inhospitable city

                                   now dying.

Jasmine (II)

Clutching the buds by the white, I
brokered brief peace in talk,

a queer species of mutterings that
attend the path toward forgiveness (the

closest to infinitude) that lies
just over a threshold you step over

but never on: a soundless procession
for what was snuffed out

like the light when you
went cold into hiding.

Some things can be flattened by rote miles,
numbered routes only known by

heart and folk song, but the rest remain
unnamable like the kind of human

love that polices itself by
knife and needle.

But the fragrance expires into
that otherwhere,

that purrs with every pleasure
you ever taught me:

those feeling times,
times of feeling.

Vanda

the orchid potted in my
               right cheek
bloomed
against expectation:
      after red's abdication

            dolorous cool
               blue
               blue currents,

surfacing
    for breath
    for recognition,
    for blue devils always do.

    so I sing to this flowering,
       juke rhythms
          pooling
          like the compounds
              whose names I cannot pronounce.

a tender opening
  into new monarchy

       purple asters that blacken
            as quickly as they are born
            the rot of blue

            even after so much care.

Weeding
After Paul Monette

you cut off my sentence which i knew was a favored strategy
a nipping in the bud of what you believe grows beneath you
soft against the hardest of your footfalls that afford no space
for deviance or even innocent error breathless until your last
but i persist like the weeds that risk outliving you that have
learned from the trampling the brutality of worn soles and
clods of dirt that do not come out willingly silently born like
the contagion you thought wiped us all out thirty years ago but
here we are daring to reclaim your space that you stole that you
borrowed but never returned because what is taken is owned
like my right to life my right to return to dust in the way i wish
lain to rest with the others you spared no mercy because pennies
are for wishing wells that don't make good on promises in a
world overseeded that it has us vying here for space only to both
lose because we are all to be rooted out some more violently

Gohyah Tea

[Case notes taken in short hand]

the hawker on the one street
without the name of a dead queen

a purgative   in a time of need,

                              bloody your feet
                                for a mouthful
of elixir

      the color of
      a fortune teller's
            nails after she
                  delivers bad news,

it burns
because for it to work
        it must be felt:
                in the throat
                in the bile

                what mothers say
                to make a bowl empty

after fires fanned,
    backs broken,
    black beans

                  come to cut
                    the taste
                    of fat
                and ferment—

                        the taste of a gourd
                            growing
                            too bitter

                            by the last sip.

Notes on a Theory of Life
After Erasmus Darwin

Is order the wrong craving if   chaos
   was always secretly the great

                first cause?
The clash
of disparate
              elements
     gave rise to organic forms
       by riveting
             atom   to   atom,
             body   to   body,

into a rude   design:

         parentless,
       spontaneous
        embryons,
       changelings
          as they move.

Simple eccentricity—
          matter's desire   swelling
               bold
           into spheres,
       lengthening into lines,
        neither hard nor fast,

but fine
enough to make itself
     a webbing of dependent
fibers ever-weaving young sensations.

          Such were the first forms, unseen
             by eye or glass,
           essays in successive life,
            a silent blooming.

But what if a form   refuses
                    this game of next?   a failure

to be fruitful, to multiply by no command
        but custom? so the line
                                breaks, as does its tyranny
a natural return
to deviant
            spontaneity
                        ripe with
                        the attractions
                        of living
                            animate pleasure.

Still Life

After Thom Gunn

Who am I to consign to
dull wax a life that refuses
to still? Living is about waxing
before the waning comes,
before the lids tighten into
murders indexing a tremor that
fruits without notice until
its warm presence insists.
Beside me, he wanders until
he finds his breath, labor in spite
of his own knack for obscurity:
a choreography of suffering in
the precise angling of his head,
arrested and reared back,
trammeled by fields of pain from
which there is no return. Only the
violation of a contract as a life-long
breather: he who must now consent
to the resignation of a mouth, one
no longer able to be shaped into its
natural, joyous O.

Crabapple

If purity is a ring,
            what happens if the body
goes pear-shaped?
            Do we reconcile with this
inevitable warping,
            born from the fingering
of the very first of us
            who had the gall to taste
beyond her imagination?
            What if the crabapple blasted
from her hand,
            its own refusal to be known,
its own refusal
            to be expelled from a paradise
of unrotting?
            The sin was never in the bite,
but in the choice
            to pick it back up.

Recovered: Vegetable Knife

The black ships anchored in the bay, and a nation
began to take on water:

ports opening like chrysanthemums
                    lining memorials for masters
whose shops would join the rest
                    of their dead
                    eating from bowls of rice
                        dusty with incense.

A warrior code
domesticated
                    into the heart of a kitchen,
a burning soothed
as it was sharpened
                        by waterstone.

Dutch frying and spicy panoplies: she still
                    took to it with her *nakiri*

because it had become
          part of her body,
          part of each body to which
                    she paid respects with
                        the execution of
                        a simple meal,

wrought in three dishes as done
before the porous days
          that mixed up words as
                    much as blood.

To cut is to recover,
                to carve histories back into
                that which will feed open mouths,
                        open hands

          after the rust of closure.

Disarmament

When the knife
pares   away

more than   skin.

Snow Chrysanthemum

A handful of chrysanthemum
blooms in under two
hundred degrees, where two
becomes one with
just a kiss of rock sugar
and wolfberries—
as do I under fine pressure
and August's heaty
garlands that encircle my
throat, already weak
with the smoke I have tried to
swallow whole.
A little spilled for him, for what
the joss paper couldn't
pay for, and what I owe those
who watch over my
chipped shoulders too busy
playing atlas to notice
the extent of the damage.
Yet these drinks to
health are but wilted buds
drained of crimson,
but sweet passing through
a painted cup.

Pithy

> *All day, all night the body intervenes.*
>
> —*Virginia Woolf*

1. I shrug off my messenger onto the floor and forget to kiss you when I walk through the door.
Pith: the pain has its steel hoop around my lumbar.

2. I catch myself tottering—a deformation of my walk.
Pith: a family resemblance: the curvature progresses faster than any other before me. I am not yet thirty.

3. I take a tumble after I miss the curb.
Pith: had you not caught me by the arm, I would have finally broken my first bone.

4. I switch positions before I even alight.
Pith: I never thought pain would claim intimacy for its own.

5. I crack three different places. It annoys you. It worries you.
Pith: they said it would make my knuckles bigger, but it is one of my most futile of pleasures.

6. I submerge myself in an epsom bath.
Pith: smelling like eucalyptus and lavender is the closest to relief because you can fool at least one of your senses.

7. I lay against you as we watch the ship go into warp.
Pith: I laid this way while doing homework all through high school, and my case silently went from light to moderate.

8. I cannot form sentences. Non-sequitur, organic hesitancy.
Pith: I would never wish upon anyone a life in the thickness of fog. The shame of being lost in it.

9. I can't make it up the stairs while cradling the box.
Pith: I hate admitting that I will have to depend on you more and more. That you will have to lie to me that it's okay.

10. I am cold and distant.
Pith: pain is subterranean, a geography to which you will forever be foreign. To be present is to also be far away.

11. I will myself to take deeper breaths. You think something is wrong.
Pith: the shallowest part of me is my breath. Some days feel breathless in all the wrong ways.

12. I look perpetually exhausted.
Pith: pain redefines what labor means.

13. I look unhappy.
Pith: joy so often feels remote, but you are teaching me that it never left me.

14. I wish it were otherwise.
Pith: magical thinking can really be cruel optimism.

15. I choose not to operate.
Pith: why should a boy ever have to choose between a life in motion or recumbence?

Yasai

a pickled moment in time
        that cuts
                through the muddled flavor of
                        worlding in progress
crisp hiatus
              before two bereavements
                    when crinkle reaches pleat
and a garden stops floating
        to collapse into the very flesh
                    of a forgiving earth
that neither dirties itself with
          vengeance of a
                  vegetal kind
a slow violence
      working through
              and upon the avenger
than toward any sweet
            justice, true and
                  earthly
nor games of deprivation
        denial of what every
                mouth knows to be plenitude
within this pot full of ferment
        there is always
                    another textured way
of forgiveness
        if only submerged until
                    found by teeth

From the Fig to the Wasp

I met your silent entrance
with tacit approval,

for I wanted the
future of you

to know the dark
of home, that sanctuary

can be sweet before
you even have to learn to fly.

You come into me to lose what
gave shape to a life:

the burden of futures,
and within me, I am multiple,

divergences mistaken as a single
fruit, when in actuality,

it is a conference of seeds
from which a proceeding emerges

out of the black and syrup
to carry the future of me into

other worlds budding quietly
in mutual nature.

Oxford

For Nolan

know that i've dreamt of you in gold
even if i don't always kiss and tell

but there you were bathed in the cold light
of the roads that wound their way

toward the farm where we almost took home
the kitten that mewed

before it realized
it would never hear its brother's crowing

a runt that we both saw ourselves in
even as we learn that strength is not survival

for the french hens gifted us
the most brittle of brown life

like the husks we pull away from ourselves
when they bind too tightly

the silken parts of us
so hidden by the chaff until they are exposed

in their goldenness that carries us
home to one another

so i continue to dream of you in gold
the very bright of our distance

full and
breathing like a beacon

Notes

"be sure to eat the skins" is for Margaret Fong. Its epigraph comes from Rosmarie Waldrop's *Driven to Abstraction* (2010).

Ikebana is the Japanese practice of flower arrangement.

"The Sick Rose" refers to a poem of the same name in William Blake's *Songs of Experience* (1794).

"Jasmine (I)" was originally published in an earlier form as "S.; or, a Retrospection" in *Unbroken*, Issue 9. Its epigraph comes from Jamie O'Neill's *At Swim, Two Boys* (2001).

Vanda is a genus in the orchid family and known for its blue color.

Gohyah tea refers to a drink made of bitter melon common in Chinese medicine.

"Notes on a Theory of Life" draws from my reading notes on Erasmus Darwin's *The Temple of Nature* (1803).

"Still Life" refers to a poem of the same name in Thom Gunn's *The Man with Night Sweats* (1992).

"Snow Chrysanthemum" was originally published in *Assaracus*, Issue 21. Snow chrysanthemum is a rare flower sometimes consumed as tea.

The epigraph to "Pithy" comes from Virginia Woolf's *On Being Ill* (1926). Number 10 makes direct reference to Elaine Scarry's *The Body In Pain* (1985).

Oxford is a city in Johnson County, Iowa.

Travis Chi Wing Lau was born in Hong Kong and currently resides in Columbus, Ohio with his partner, Nolan, and rescue cat, Mercury. He completed his Ph.D. in English at the University of Pennsylvania and currently serves as Assistant Professor of Eighteenth-Century and Romantic British Literature at Kenyon College. His research and teaching focuses on the intersections of eighteenth- and nineteenth-century British literature, health humanities, and disability studies. He is currently completing his first academic monograph, *Insecure Immunity: Inoculation and Anti-Vaccination, 1720-1898*, which explores the British cultural history of vaccination. Lau has published in *Disability Studies Quarterly, Journal of Literary & Cultural Disability Studies, Eighteenth-Century Fiction*, as well as in venues for public scholarship like *Public Books, Lapham's Quarterly*, and *The Los Angeles Review of Books*. His poetry centers around issues of embodiment, particularly experiences of chronic pain and disability as they are inflected by his queer and Asian American identities. Travis's poems have been published in *Nat. Brut., District Lit, Impossible Archetype, A&U Magazine, Foglifter, Barren Magazine*, and *The South Carolina Review*. Several of his works have been nominated for The Puschart Prize and *Best of the Net*, as well as anthologized in *Lovejets: Queer Male Poets on 200 Years of Walt Whitman* and in *My Loves: A Digital Anthology of Queer Love Poems*. His first chapbook, *The Bone Setter*, was released in 2019 with Damaged Goods Press. [travisclau.com]

CPSIA information can be obtained
at www.ICGtesting.com
Printed in the USA
LVHW091915140121
676491LV00015B/668

9 781646 623747